Hymns Of The Heart

From a lost soul

Tara

India | USA | UK

Copyright © Tara
All Rights Reserved.

This book has been self-published with all reasonable efforts taken to make the material error-free by the author. No part of this book shall be used, reproduced in any manner whatsoever without written permission from the author, except in the case of brief quotations embodied in critical articles and reviews.

The Author of this book is solely responsible and liable for its content including but not limited to the views, representations, descriptions, statements, information, opinions, and references ["Content"]. The Content of this book shall not constitute or be construed or deemed to reflect the opinion or expression of the Publisher or Editor. Neither the Publisher nor Editor endorse or approve the Content of this book or guarantee the reliability, accuracy, or completeness of the Content published herein and do not make any representations or warranties of any kind, express or implied, including but not limited to the implied warranties of merchantability, fitness for a particular purpose.

The Publisher and Editor shall not be liable whatsoever...

Made with ♥ on the BookLeaf Publishing Platform
www.bookleafpub.in
www.bookleafpub.com

Dedication

**To the one who once held my heart.
Thank you for the cracks, through them, I learned to grow light.**

Preface

A Note to the Heart That's Hurting

When I began writing these
poems,
I believed I was placing a broken
piece of my heart on every page
piece after piece,
hurt after hurt
convinced that by the final poem,
there would be nothing left of me
to mend.
But somewhere along the
journey,

I realized something
unexpected...
I wasn't scattering the pieces of
my heart,
I was stitching them back
together.
With every word I wrote,
I reclaimed a part of myself
I thought was gone forever.
I hope the same happens for you.
Don't rush through the pages.
Don't run from the ache.
Let every poem lead you gently
through what hurts
because you cannot heal

without walking through the
pain.
And by the time you reach the
end,
may you discover what I did:
you were putting yourself back
together
all along.

Acknowledgements

To the nights that hurt.
To the mornings that healed.
To the love that ended
and the self that began.
Without that heartbreak,
this book would have never been
born.

Waiting on the Swing

I sit on this swing, the chains creak slow,
Beneath my laughter, is a storm they don't know.
A weight unseen, a burden I bear,
Yearning for someone who'll truly care.

Through the quiet smiles with bright-eyed disguise,
I hide the tears that never rise.

But I wait, for the one with
gentle piercing sight,
Who'll see the shadows behind
the light.

Will he come, with steady hands,
To lift my heart, to understand?
To whisper softly, "I'm here,
you're free,
Rest your soul, lean into me."

The little girl swings, waiting
still,
With hopes that one day, she'll
find the will,

To share the silence, the heaviness there,
With someone who will truly care.

I hope her wait ends when he appears,
And says, "Relax, my love, I'm here."

The Melody of One

The anklet gleams in silver light,
A single chain, so soft, so bright.
Its jingles hum, a tender sound,
Yet something lost cannot be found.

It dances with the evening breeze,
A gentle song, a whispered tease.
But in its notes, a hollow rings,

For where's the pair that balance brings?

Alone it shines, but feels the lack,
The echo of the missing track.
For two together fill the air
With harmony beyond compare.

Though it sparkles on its own,
It dreams of steps not walked alone.
A melody of one may sing,
But two are where the heart takes wing.

Beneath The Surface

Don't tell me I'm strong when I share my sorrow,
I wasn't strong; just had no choice but to borrow
Strength from the silence when no shoulder was near,
So I clung to my pillow and waited for dawn to appear.

When you see me flying on wings that are torn,

Don't say I can rise, don't speak of being reborn.
I wanted perfect wings, but the storms broke me down,
And I longed for the wind, yet none could be found.

When you see me laugh through the tears in my eyes,
Don't say I'm brave, those are hollow replies.
I wanted to cry, but had no hands to wipe the stream,
So I laughed, and I flew, hiding behind dreams.

I am not strong, don't mistake it for might.
I just had no option, no choice but the fight.

The Last That Never Was

I search my mind, a stormy sea,
For the last hug, the last kiss, the final "we."
But memory slips, a thief in the night,
And leaves me grasping at fading light.

I never knew, as arms entwined,
That time would render love confined.

That kiss, so soft, unmarked by fate,
Would stand as the silent closing gate.

Had I known, oh, had I guessed,
I would have wrapped that moment in my chest
A treasure bound by threads of care,
To hold forever, to never tear.

But God, perhaps, in wisdom wise,
Hid the truth beneath the skies.

For hearts would cling, would never mend,
If we knew where every story ends.

A Simple Wish

I didn't want much from life, just a simple embrace,
The sweet fragrance of jasmine in a sunlit space.
Bangles that chime with a gentle sound,
Anklets that tinkle as they twirl around.

Love like the breeze, soft and free,

Laughter that echoes in harmony.
No riches, no gold, no grander scheme,
Just moments of joy, like a sweet dream.

A heart that beats with tender care,
In a world where smiles are everywhere.
That's all I wished, nothing more,
A life of peace, love at its core.

I Wonder, Do You Care?

I wonder, do you care,
If I reach home before the stars settle,
Or if the night swallows me whole,
Would it matter, to you, at all?

I wonder, is there someone out there,
Who would frown at my empty plate,

Who would sigh if I forget my pills,
Who would pull me close and say, "Take care"?

If sleep wraps me too tight,
Or if I never wake up to see the sun,
Would it make your heart ache,
Or would my absence be just another passing shadow?

I wonder, is there a soul,
Who would cradle my heart in steady hands,

Who would whisper, "Stay whole, my love,"
And guard the innocence I fear to lose?

Is there a love that stands like a shield,
That fights against the cruel hands of time,
That sees me truly, deeply, as I am,
And stays, even when the world forgets?

I wonder, do you exist?

Somewhere, in this vast and weary world
A love not fleeting, not careless, not cruel,
But a love that simply... cares.

The Fake Ring

You slipped a fake ring onto my finger,
and I, lost in love, waited for magic,
for time to turn illusion into truth.
But love does not alchemize deceit,
and now I see, my worth to you,
was just as hollow as the promise
you never meant to keep.

Loving You Alone

How did you forget me so easily?
Like a stray seed caught in the wind,
gone with the faintest breath,
while I remained, bound to you,
woven into every inhale,
every exhale, every thought.

When I couldn't forget you...
You were everywhere.
In the echoes of my laughter,

in the weight of my anger,
in the salt of my tears.
You lived in the spaces between
my ribs,
in the silence before I slept,
in the prayers I whispered
but never had answered.

Why couldn't you see it was
always you?
Every gaze, every word, every
wound,
they all traced back to you.
I made you my sun,

but you let me drown in
darkness,
never once turning back
to see me reaching for the light.

Why was I not enough?
When you were all I ever
wanted,
when I folded my soul into your
hands,
when I would have given the
world
if you had just asked.

Why was I not enough for you?

When you were everything to me.
When you filled my every prayer,
but I never even touched yours.

Why couldn't I just be a part of your world?
Was I always meant to love from afar,
watching you build your life
as if I had never been in it?
Was I only a passing season,
a fleeting warmth you forgot,
while you remained my endless winter?

I Wish You Knew

I wish all the stars could whisper
to you,
the story of each tear I shed,
how they fell, silent and unseen,
yet carried the weight of all I left
unsaid.

I wish your ego was smaller than
your love,
that pride had not stood in love's
way.

I wish you had come to marry me again,
  as fast as you walked away.

I wish you could see the pain still here,
  woven into every breath I take.
I wish you could read my silent prayers,
  where your name still lingers, wide awake.

I wish you could see the thoughts I hold,

each one carved with your name inside.
I wish you could see my searching eyes,
waiting for you in every tide.

But wishes are whispers in an empty room,
echoes that fade into the night.
And you, you're just a shadow now,
too far to hear, too lost to fight.

The Witness

I do not seek a fleeting flame,
A kiss that fades, a whispered name.
I yearn for eyes that see me whole,
The silent keeper of my soul.

Let others chase the rush, the race,
The perfect smile, the flawless face.

I ache for love that dares to stay,
Through quiet night and weary day.

A heart that knows the weight I bear,
That sees my scars and still stays there.
Not to fix or turn away,
But simply, choose to always stay.

To walk beside me, step by step,
Through chapters no one else has read.

To laugh when joy spills over light,
To hold me close through sleepless nights.

I long for love that takes its time,
That holds the pauses in the rhyme.
That witnesses my rise and fall,
And softly says, "I've seen it all."

Not loud, not grand, just deeply true,
A soul that says, I see you through.

Until the end, and past the end,
A lover, witness, guide, and friend.

So Near, Yet So Far

I ran out of excuses to see you again,
Each reason felt borrowed, each visit in vain.
You gave me no answer, no soft little sign,
No whispered hello to say you were mine.

You never once asked, "Will you come today?"

No message, no moment to make me stay.
I stood on the edge of a maybe, a when,
But silence was louder than we ever had been.

Are we forgotten, just like a dream?
Like winter erased by a sunbeam's gleam?
Were we a pause, a fleeting delay,
A story misplaced and swept away?

I envy the souls stretched over the skies,
Who love through the distance, who never need lies.
Their hearts still beat, no matter how far,
While I reach for you through an invisible scar.

You're close in the map, a street or a two,
But you feel like the stars, too distant to view.
So near I could touch, yet far as the moon,

We faded away far too early, too soon.

The Distance Between Our Breaths

I got tired of waiting for you to look at me with love,
Eyes meeting mine, but never deep enough.
I stood in silence, hoping you'd hear
The echo of my ache, ringing clear.

I got tired of waiting for you to see my pain,

The quiet storms, the steady rain.
You held my hand, but not my heart,
Together in body, but always apart.

I got tired of waiting to feel your care,
Of finding emptiness in places I thought you were there.
Our breath still mingles in the quiet night,
Yet our souls drift like ships out of sight.

Ocean wide, this silence grows,
A love unspoken, a truth that shows.
I don't know how to close this space,
To find again that missing grace.

I've built bridges out of words and tears,
Out of all my hopes and hidden fears.
But still, I stand on the other side,
Waving at a love that's learned to hide.

And now I ask, what more to do,
When I've broken myself just reaching you?
Even love, when left unheard,
Becomes a faded, aching word.

Invisible

It came like a hush on a noisy day,
A truth I had dodged in every way.
Not with a scream, not with a storm,
Just silence dressed in quiet form.

You will never see me,never had.
I was a flicker, a phase, a passing fad.

Not because I wasn't loud enough,
But because to you, I wasn't ever enough.

I painted skies in words for you,
Stood at the edge of hope, so true.
Thinking maybe, if I waited long,
You'd turn, you'd look I would belong.

But I am the wind you never feel,
The echo lost beneath your heels.

I gave you chapters you never
read,
A heart too loud, too full, too red.

It's not hate, it's not despair,
Just the ache of loving air.
Of chasing shadows, chasing
dreams,
That only lived inside my seams.

So I let go, not in rage or spite,
But in the softness of the night.
It's a quiet end, not loud or
grand,

Just me, unclenching a desperate hand.

Because sometimes love is just a ghost,
A fire that dies in the one who loves most.
And I, I was only ever the breeze,
Wishing to be your storm. But now, I cease.

Why Won't You Call?

Why won't you call?
Is my silence not loud enough to
reach you,
Like yours, tears through me like
a storm?
Don't you feel this ache,
This quiet breaking,
That keeps my heart awake in
your name?

Do you think of me

Like I think of you,
In the spaces between seconds,
In the stillness between breaths,
Where every thought is you,
And every thought hurts?

It's so painful
To think of you,
But more so not to.
You live in me,
A thousand times a day,
While I wonder
If I even pass your mind at all.

Don't you care

What today did to me?
The wars I fought with a smile,
The way I swallowed the world
Hoping you'd ask
If I made it through?

I carry your pain
Like it's my own.
But when mine screams,
Do you even hear?

Why am I
Not your everything,
When you
Are all I breathe for?

Why won't you call?
Isn't love supposed to echo
Both ways?

Disconnected

I couldn't sleep today,
felt like the cord was cut,
like silence settled where your name
once echoed in the hush of dusk.

No tether to the place we met,
no warmth left in the dark,
just the cold hum of absence,
and a sky that forgot how to spark.

Sleep didn't come tonight,
perhaps it knew before I did,
that you wouldn't be waiting
in that quiet dream where we
once hid.

No longer yours to find me there,
no longer mine to stay,
a vanished hand, a fading face,
the night just turned away.

And I, left staring through the
dark,
knew what it meant to lose,

not in waking,
but in the one place I thought I couldn't.

The Right to Dream

And you faded a little bit more
today,
like twilight slipping beneath the
sea,
soft, inevitable,
and far from me.

I cried into the night,
after such a long quiet stretch
where I fooled myself
into believing I had healed.

Silent cries,
big tears,
the kind that ache
not from presence,
but the echo of your absence.

Because now I know,
truly know,
that I no longer have the right
to dream about you again.

Not when you've left the realm of maybe,
not when you've slipped

from memory into myth.

Tonight,
my tears baptized the truth,
even dreams
must let go of you.

Not Meant for Smaller Things

I don't know why I didn't see,
The calls won't come, they're not for me.
No tether links these hearts of two,
No path remains to wander together through.

So I have learnt to let the waiting cease,

To let silent nights become my peace.
No strings connect what's not aligned,
No love to pull, no ties to bind.

Released the tears I held so tight,
They've done their time, I have earned the night.
It wasn't fate, just what it is,
A fleeting touch, a moment's kiss.

Taking it as a gift, not loss,
A friend, not meant to be my cross.

Just a friend, no more, no less,
A soul that came and brought a bless.

But I, I know, am built for more,
Not scraps of love or closing doors.
I am burning slow, but I will shine,
A quiet spark, by grand design.

I wasn't made for smaller things,
But skies and stars and fire with wings.

So I will rise and glow, time will show,
The light I have was meant to grow.

The Ball

There's a ball inside my chest
not of light,
but of weight.

It coils in silence,
tight with fear,
a tangle of thoughts
I cannot name
but cannot escape.

It rolls through my day,

follows me to bed,
sits on my breath
like a storm
I've learned to swallow.

No one sees it
how could they?
I smile.
I function.
But inside,
I carry
the ball.

And some days,
I wish

someone would just say,
"You can put it down now. I'll hold it with you."

Why Couldn't I Be Your Centre?

And you left me standing
with all the dreams, all alone,
their fragile wings trembling
in the quiet air you left behind.

I gathered them gently,
every half-formed promise,
every echo of your name,
as if holding them could bring
you back.

You became my sun,
my centre of the universe.
I moved around you,
drawn by a warmth that burned
and healed me all at once.

I timed my breaths to your
laughter,
measured my days by your
moods,
believed that love was gravity
and I was meant to fall.

But you never looked my way.
I was a distant planet,

turning faithfully in your light,
while you kept chasing other
skies.

You never saw how my world
tilted toward you,
how every dawn was just
another way
of calling your name.

Why couldn't I be your centre?
Was I too quiet, too steady,
too much of what you never
needed?

I would have carried your storms,
softened your edges,
been the calm you never knew
you wanted.
But you were already gone,
long before your footsteps faded.

Now I walk through your
absence
like an old house with all its
lights turned off.
Every corner still remembers
the way you once fit into the air.

And though I keep telling myself

to find another orbit,
my heart still drifts,
forever caught
in the pull of your impossible
sun.

The Day I Stop

One day,
I will not check the screen
like a pilgrim waiting for a
miracle.
I will not measure my worth
by the weight of your silence.

One day,
my fingers will rest quietly
instead of trembling over your
name,

and the hours will pass
without the ache to fill them with
you.

One day,
my heart will feel like home
again,
walls painted in my own colors,
rooms filled with laughter
that does not echo your absence.

One day,
I will wake up,
and your ghost will no longer
sleep beside me.

That day,
I will call freedom by my name.

21. The Hardest Work

The hardest work is not the climb,
It's standing when the ground still sways beneath you,
When the dust of your fall clings to your bones,
And your knees remember the weight of breaking.

It's wearing a smile like armor,

Laughing loud enough to drown the sob
That beats inside your throat every second,
Faking sunlight until, one day,
It feels a little warmer than before.

The hardest part is keeping your heart tender
When life has carved it with rough hands,
Still planting softness like wildflowers
So the world around you

Doesn't turn as sharp as the
world within.

And hardest of all,
To offer trust again,
To cradle faith in trembling
palms
Even after it's slipped through
your fingers
A hundred times.

Yet somehow,
You stand.
You smile.
You love.

And in that quiet, stubborn grace,
You win.

www.ingramcontent.com/pod-product-compliance
Lightning Source LLC
Chambersburg PA
CBHW060347050426
42449CB00011B/2864